The Easy Way to Improve Your Golf
With S/A Golf Hypnotism

By Don Diebel

Copyright © 2009 by Gemini Publishing Company

Gemini Publishing Company
818 Lois Street, Suite A
Kerrville, TX 78028
Website: http://www.getgirls.com

TABLE OF CONTENTS

Introduction

Did you ever wonder why it is that some golfers have absolutely no trouble making good shots while others find it most difficult?

And does this describe you?

1. You spend a fortune buying and trying golf clubs to improve your game.
2. You spend money on expensive golf lessons.
3. You spend hours on the driving range and putting green.
4. You subscribe to all the golf magazines to get tips on how to improve your game.
5. You buy golf books, videos, CD's, and DVD's.
6. You buy all the devices, gadgets, and accessories you see in the golf stores, golf magazines, info-commercials, and Ebay to improve your game.
7. Also, you buy the expensive golf balls that the pros use.

And after doing all this, your game is still inconsistent. You never know what to expect from one game to the next or from one hole to the next. You just can't seem to get over the hump and you are so frustrated. You can't seem to figure out what in the hell is wrong.

Well there is a rather simple explanation for this. You see...it takes a bit of confidence to play good golf. Confidence in yourself. Confidence in your skills.

Take any golfer who is on top of his game...and you'll find that he has all the confidence and self-assurance in the world. This type of golfer has a "positive self-image" on the golf course.

Some golfers just naturally possess the quality of self-confidence. And they put it to use whenever they're on the course. They let it work for them every time they hit the ball. They have learned to rely on it. And it seldom lets them down.

On the other hand: Some golfers are not naturally in possession of this priceless asset of self-confidence and positive self-image...and therefore must find a way to change their negative self-image and lack of confidence in their skills to one of a positive nature.

Through S/A Golf Hypnotism, you will be able to develop more than enough confidence to improve your game. Once you acquire this new inner-confidence, you will find it extremely easy to make shots you never thought you could, hit the ball long, high, and straight down the middle of the fairway, cut 5-10-15 strokes off your handicap, and take your game to the next level. THAT'S WHAT S/A GOLF HYPNOTISM CAN DO FOR YOU!

How Would Like to:

1.   Hit your ball longer and straighter than you ever thought possible?
2.   Get rid of your slice once and for all?
3.   Take your game to the next level?
4.   Hit your driver an extra 30 yards?
5.   Putt like a pro and effortlessly sink those impossible putts and watch your ball be magnetically drawn to the cup?
6.   Hit all your chip and pitch shots dead on the pin from 100 yards in?
7.   Hit all your tee shots long and straight down the middle of the fairway?

8.	Lower your handicap 5-10-15 strokes?
9.	Hit your driver, fairway woods, long irons better?
10.	Hit all your shots with pinpoint accuracy?

These are just some of the benefits available to the golfer who has a "positive self-image" and supreme confidence in his game. And these are the benefits that will be available to YOU...once you develop your own positive self-image and confidence through S/A Golf Hypnotism.

Keep in mind as you read - we are not talking mere theory or giving you our opinions. We are giving you COLD HARD FACTS!

CHAPTER ONE

S/A Golf Hypnotism - What Is It?

S/A Golf Hypnotism is self-administered hypnotism. It is also known as autosuggestion or simply called self-hypnotism. But they all add up to basically the same thing: Hypnotism performed BY yourself...ON yourself...for the purpose of replacing certain negative qualities in your golf game with those of a positive, more desirable nature.

S/A Golf Hypnotism and the Subconscious Mind

"We are what we "think" we are."

Read that sentence again. Think about it. It's quite true. We truly ARE what we THINK we are.

If you don't "think" you can make that ten-foot putt, you probably won't.

If you don't "think" you can hit the fairway, you probably won't make it.

If you don't "think" you can make that golf shot, YOU PROBABLY WON'T!

But it's a little more than merely thinking about it. You must honestly BELIEVE. Believe in yourself. Believe that you will at least par every hole you play. Believe that you will hit the ball long and straight down the fairway. Believe that you always hit the green from 150 yards out. . . etc.

If playing with others, before you can beat the other guys at golf you must actually believe you are the best golfer on the course and can't be beat.

And before you can expect to be a low handicap golfer, you must honestly "believe" you have that certain "something" that makes you a great golfer. You must believe it with all your heart.

Then...and only then...will you become the successful golfer you have always wanted to be.

The Magic of Believing

QUESTION: How do you "believe with all your heart" that you're a great golfer who consistently makes all his shots?

ANSWER: You lead your subconscious mind to believe it.

YOU AUTOMATICALLY TURN INTO THE
TYPE OF SUPER GOLFER THAT YOUR
SUBCONSCIOUS MIND BELIEVES YOU ARE

Once your subconscious mind believes you are a great golfer who consistently pars or better on every hole, a golfer who consistently makes his shots, hits the fairway, hits the greens and takes only two putts or less to get the ball in the hole, your conscious mind will begin to believe it. And once this begins to happen, you will automatically come into possession of that all-important "self confidence." Which in turn, leads you directly to the success on the course that you've always wanted.

Remember - we guarantee your success. But you must give it an honest try. If you do just that much, the principles described in this audio book will lead you directly to be the great low handicap golfer you have always wanted to be. BUT YOU MUST TRY!

Making Your Subconscious Mind "Believe"

Through S/A Golf Hypnotism, you will be able to give your subconscious mind "suggestions." After a short time (it could take a few weeks, a week, or only a couple of days), your subconscious mind will begin to believe the information that you have been feeding it and will finally accept it as "truth."

At that time when your subconscious takes the suggestions you've been giving it as "truth," a change will immediately take place in your conscious mind and, thus, in your every-day way of thinking (and playing golf).

Example: There is a very popular heavyweight fighter who turned to self-hypnotism for aid when the going got rough. For years he was just another pug. Then he began to practice the techniques we are about to teach you.

Through these techniques, he was easily able to reach his subconscious mind...at which time he gave it certain suggestions with the hope that he would be "lifted" to the level of greatness that produces champions.

IT WORKED. His subconscious responded to the suggestions that were given to it.

Before long, he was beating every opponent he came up against. With the help of self-hypnotism, he climbed that steep ladder of success WITH EASE. And he kept on climbing until at last...he became the number one contender for the heavyweight championship of the world!!!

Does S/A Golf Hypnotism work?

You bet it does!

These principles have helped countless men achieve success in their own particular calling. And...these very principles will help you become a better golfer. Before long, your golf buddies will stare in amazement at all the great shots you make.

Remember - we guarantee it will work for you IF you give it an honest try.

And remember also - there is not hard work involved. The basic simple formula you will be following is this: 1) Reach your subconscious mind through S/A Golf Hypnotism, then 2) give your subconscious certain "suggestions" that will (after a short period of time) be accepted as "truth" by your subconscious as well as your conscious mind (at which time, 3) you will automatically become the golfer that you are commanding your subconscious mind to help you become.

Don't worry if you don't understand exactly WHY these principles work. The important thing is that you accept the fact that they DO work.

CHAPTER TWO

Preparing Your Subconscious
Mind to Receive Suggestions

Warning...do not listen to this audio book while driving or operating machinery

Before you can give your subconscious mind suggestions, you must "prepare" it to receive them. This is known as: putting yourself in an altered-consciousness. Let us Begin.

Procedure #1

Retire to a quiet room free from any outside disturbances. This room will require enough light so you can listen and be dark enough for a comfortable and relaxing atmosphere.

Relax by stretching out on a bed or in your favorite easy chair. It is suggested that you do not lie entirely flat. Just prop your head and shoulders on a couple of pillows.

Now, get comfortable and relaxed. Close your eyes and relax. Relax every single muscle in your body.

Now, blank your mind of all thoughts. Simply relax...and think of nothing at all. Block all outside noises and distractions completely from your mind. Keep your eyes closed.

Procedure #2

Now, you will silently command each and every part of your body to relax (be sure and actually feel each body-part totally relax as you give each command).

1. Command your feet to relax (take your time and actually feel them relaxing).
2. Command your ankles to relax.
3. Command your calves to relax (feel the muscles in your calves relaxing).
4. Command your knees to relax.
5. Command your thighs to relax (feel every muscle in your thighs relaxing).

*** NOTE - Don't Rush...Take Your Time Between Each Command**

6. Command your stomach to relax (feel your stomach muscles relaxing).
7. Command your chest muscles to relax (feel them relaxing).
8. Command your shoulders to relax (feel them relaxing).
9. Command your upper arms to relax.
10. Command your elbows to relax.
11. Command your forearms to relax.
12. Command your wrists to relax.
13. Command your hands to relax (feel each finger and joint in your hands relaxing).
14. Command your lower back to relax.
15. Command your upper back to relax (feel all the muscles in your upper and lower back relaxing).
16. Command all the muscles in the back of your neck to relax (feel them relaxing).
17. Command the back of your head and scalp to relax.
18. Command all the muscles in your face to relax (feel your eyes, mouth, cheeks, etc. relaxing).
19. Command your entire body to relax (actually feel all your muscles, joints, nerves and mind totally relax).

At this point, your entire body should be in a completely relaxed state. Also, your mind should be completely relaxed and completely free from all thought. You should be thinking of nothing.

Procedure #3

Now, you will relax your mind and body even more.

With your eyes still closed...with your mind blank...and with every muscle in your body totally relaxed, begin to count from 1 to 20 slowly.

As you count, tell yourself that your mind and body are becoming more and more relaxed.

As you count 1-2-3-4, feel your mind and body becoming more relaxed.

As you count 5-6-7-8-9-10-11-12-13-14-15-16, feel yourself going into a deeper and deeper state of relaxation.

As you count 17-18-19 and finally 20, tell yourself (and actually FEEL) that you are now in a very relaxed, almost sleep-like condition - with your mind and body totally relaxed and your mind completely free of all worry, emotions, problems, etc. Think of absolutely nothing!

NOTE: Do not use these principles real late at night or when you are real tired. By doing so, you may easily fall asleep and (this is something you do not want to happen).

The best time to practice S/A Golf Hypnotism is mid-morning, mid-afternoon, or evening.

You are now ready to give your subconscious mind suggestions. But first, it is important for you to learn a little about the suggestions themselves before you actually put them into action.

CHAPTER THREE

The "Suggestions"

Suggestions are nothing more than ideas handed over to your subconscious mind. The manner in which this is done may seem a little strange to you. Just keep an open mind. If you will just give these principles a chance, they will work for you to improve your golf game dramatically!

To begin with, all suggestions are put forth in a present, positive, first-person manner.

Example: If you happened to be in training to become the heavyweight champion of the world, you would not say to yourself, "I will become the greatest heavyweight fighter of all time."

Instead, you would say to yourself: "I am the greatest heavyweight fighter of all time."

The difference between the two may not seem that important to you. BUT, BELIEVE ME, IT IS! That little difference in wording holds the key to improving your golf.

Example: Let's say that one of your hang-ups is hitting slices...and you want to use S/A Golf Hypnotism to correct this problem.

OK - now if you worded the suggestion to say: "I will cure my slice by no longer hitting the ball with an out-to-in swing path and my clubface is not open at impact," "IT WILL NOT WORK! Why?

First of all, when you say, "I will cure my slice," you are reminding yourself that you are presently uncomfortable with your shots. This will have a negative effect on your subconscious mind and is simply wrong.

The "Suggestions"

Secondly, when you say, "I will cure my slice," you are delaying the time when you will receive any positive results...When will you cure your slice? Next week? Next month? Next year?

So, if you want to get positive results right now...simply change the wording of the suggestion to: "I am now curing my slice by no longer hitting the ball with an out-to-in swing path and my clubface is not open at impact."

Mix in Feeling and Emotion

Take the above example: "I am now curing my slice by no longer hitting the ball with an out-to-in swing path and my clubface is not open at impact."

This suggestion is worded correctly...but it isn't quite enough to merely say the words to yourself. When giving suggestions to the subconscious mind, you must mix in a little "feeling" or emotion. This is very important.

For example - when you say to yourself, "I am now curing my slice," actually form a picture in your mind's eye of you hitting the ball long, high, and straight toward the target. SEE yourself hitting the ball with an in-to-out swing path and the clubface is always square to the target at impact.

Do this...and the next time you are in a real life situation on the golf course you won't hit slices anymore.

Just have faith in these principles and have faith in yourself. Believe that these principles will work for you, and they won't let you down. Do your part and (practice S/A Golf Hypnotism faithfully), and nature will do the rest.

CHAPTER FOUR

Putting S/A Golf Hypnotism Into Action

We will now continue from where we left off at the end of Chapter Two.

Your mind and body should now be completely relaxed and totally "prepared" to receive suggestions.

You should be going from Procedures 1-3 in Chapter Two directly to Procedure #1 below:

Procedure #1

Open your eyes long enough to say the following suggestion. Say it to yourself a few times...

"I now hit all my shots higher, straighter, and longer and the ball lands exactly where I want it to."

Now ...close your eyes and repeat the suggestion to yourself several more times...WITH BELIEF!

As you say the suggestion to yourself, SEE yourself hitting the ball high, straight, long and landing exactly where you want it to. FEEL yourself hitting the ball high, straight, long and watch it land exactly where you want it to. BELIEVE that all the shots you hit are high, straight, long and land exactly where you want them to.

Procedure #2

Open your eyes just long enough to say the next suggestion. Read it a few times.

"Before I take a shot, I always visualize hitting the perfect shot. In my mind I see and feel the ball launching off the clubface and going high in the air heading dead on target"

Now close your eyes and repeat the previous suggestion to yourself several more times. And...as before...repeat it to yourself with belief.

As you say the previous suggestion to yourself, SEE yourself hitting the perfect shot. Actually see the ball launching off the clubface and going high in the air right to the target. FEEL yourself being totally self-confident and self-assured when you make your shots knowing that it will be one of the best shots you've ever made. BELIEVE that you actually do have all the confidence and self-assurance to make great shots that will make your golf buddies envious.

Procedure #3

Go through the remaining suggestions we have listed below on this page, following the same procedure as outlined above and pick out the ones that fit your needs to improve your golf game.
I would recommend writing them down on a piece of paper the ones that you need.

NOTE: It is important that you use the SEE...FEEL...BELIEVE technique for each suggestion. This is the only way you will be able to reach your subconscious mind, and thus, receive positive results.

NOTE: You are to open your eyes between each suggestion ONLY until they are memorized. Once memorized, simply keep your eyes closed throughout the entire procedure. You should memorize the suggestions as soon as possible...as it will be more beneficial to you to keep your eyes closed throughout the entire procedure.

NOTE: do not get discouraged if you find it somewhat awkward (in the beginning) when trying to "see" - "feel" - and - "believe" each suggestion. This is to be expected. Don't worry about it.

You will become more and more at ease with these principles each day that you practice them.

Your Remaining Daily Suggestions

I have absolutely no limitations when it comes to improving my golf game.

It is extremely easy for me to hit the green from 150 yards or less.

I have absolutely no fear of any bunker and I easily get up & down from any bunker and can play any sand shot from any lie.

I have cured my slice by no longer hitting the ball with an out-to-in swing path and my clubface is not open at impact.

My failure days with my chip and pitch shots are gone forever and my chip and pitch shots are now dead on the pin.

I am able to hit every tee shot long and straight down the middle of the fairway.

I don't panic when I have to make a shot to clear the water. I just forget about the water and pretend it's just grass there and confidently hit the ball with my normal rhythm and swing.

I always hit the ball with the clubface square to the target.

I am able to add 20-40 yards to my tee shots.

I am improving my game by not trying to steer my club into the ball, instead I concentrate on swinging the club head toward the target.

I am devoting most of my time to my short game instead of being obsessed with trying to see how far I can hit my driver.

When I hit my driver, I am now keeping my left arm as straight as possible on the backswing to ensure a wide swing arc.

My left elbow stays tucked in during my follow-through to achieve pinpoint accuracy.

I always have my club head in the perfect position upon impact with the ball.

My alignment is always perfect because I always line up the clubface square to the target and my feet, hips and shoulders are lined up parallel to the clubface.

I am now improving my iron shots by striking the ball with a slightly descending blow with the club brushing or nipping the turf after contacting the ball.

When at the driving range I focus hard on each shot and pick out a target. By picking out a target this helps my game when I get on the course.

I don't wish I could hit the fairway anymore. I now pick out where I want the ball to land on the fairway and nail it every time!

I always focus on the target and create a vivid picture of where I want the ball to go during my pre-shot routine.

I always approach every bunker shot with the deep gut feeling that I'm going to knock the ball into the hole. Bunker shots don't scare me and never will!

I am in total control of my emotions on the golf course. I don't lose my temper when I make a bad shot. I stay calm and focused and picture my next shot as one of the best shots I've ever hit.

When I'm at the driving range I trick my mind into thinking I'm in a game situation. I pretend I'm on the course and try to hit the perfect shot.

I have developed a pre-swing waggle that eases tension before striking the ball. This creates nerves of steel for me.

I am able to ice business deals with clients while playing golf.

Whenever I hit a shot, I am totally free from all negative feelings...such as worry, nervousness, or lack of confidence.

Procedure #4

After completing your daily suggestions, remain relaxed. Remain in the same position and relax your whole body.

Think of nothing...keep your eyes closed...and relax.
Relax...relax...relax...relax and enjoy it...relax...

After two or three minutes of this you will be ready to
come out of S/A Golf Hypnotism.

ink of nothing...keep your eyes closed...and relax.
lax...relax...relax...relax and enjoy it...relax...

fter two or three minutes of this you will be ready to
me out of S/A Golf Hypnotism.

will be more beneficial to you to keep your eyes closed
throughout the entire procedure.

NOTE: do not get discouraged if you find it somewhat
awkward (in the beginning) when trying to "see" - "feel" -
and - "believe" each suggestion. This is to be expected.
Don't worry about it.

You will become more and more at ease with these
principles each day that you practice them.

Your Remaining Daily Suggestions

I have absolutely no limitations when it comes to
improving my golf game.

It is extremely easy for me to hit the green from 150 yards
or less.

I have absolutely no fear of any bunker and I easily get up
& down from any bunker and can play any sand shot from
any lie.

I have cured my slice by no longer hitting the ball with an
out-to-in swing path and my clubface is not open at impact.

My failure days with my chip and pitch shots are gone
forever and my chip and pitch shots are now dead on the
pin.

I am able to hit every tee shot long and straight down the
middle of the fairway.

I don't panic when I have to make a shot to clear the water.
I just forget about the water and pretend it's just grass there

and confidently hit the ball with my normal rhythm and swing.

I always hit the ball with the clubface square to the target.

I am able to add 20-40 yards to my tee shots.

I am improving my game by not trying to steer my club into the ball, instead I concentrate on swinging the club head toward the target.

I am devoting most of my time to my short game instead of being obsessed with trying to see how far I can hit my driver.

When I hit my driver, I am now keeping my left arm as straight as possible on the backswing to ensure a wide swing arc.

My left elbow stays tucked in during my follow-through to achieve pinpoint accuracy.

I always have my club head in the perfect position upon impact with the ball.

My alignment is always perfect because I always line up the clubface square to the target and my feet, hips and shoulders are lined up parallel to the clubface.

I am now improving my iron shots by striking the ball with a slightly descending blow with the club brushing or nipping the turf after contacting the ball.

When at the driving range I focus hard on each shot and pick out a target. By picking out a target this helps my game when I get on the course.

I don't wish I could hit the fairway anymore. out where I want the ball to land on the fairw every time!

I always focus on the target and create a vivic where I want the ball to go during my pre-sho

I always approach every bunker shot with the feeling that I'm going to knock the ball into tl Bunker shots don't scare me and never will!

I am in total control of my emotions on the gc don't lose my temper when I make a bad shot and focused and picture my next shot as one c shots I've ever hit.

When I'm at the driving range I trick my minc thinking I'm in a game situation. I pretend I'm course and try to hit the perfect shot.

I have developed a pre-swing waggle that ease before striking the ball. This creates nerves of

I am able to ice business deals with clients wh golf.

Whenever I hit a shot, I am totally free from al feelings...such as worry, nervousness, or lack c confidence.

Procedure #4

After completing your daily suggestions, remai Remain in the same position and relax your wh

CHAPTER FIVE

Coming Out of S/A Golf Hypnotism

The "coming out" phase of S/A Golf Hypnotism is just as important as any other part.

When you come out of S/A Golf Hypnotism correctly (in the manner which we are about to teach you), you instantly feel much better (physically as well as mentally) than you did before you started the session. You will feel greatly refreshed and rested. You will feel more alert, energetic, confident and self-assured. You will truly feel like a new man!

Procedure #1

With your eyes still closed...and your mind totally blank...start counting backwards from 20 down to 1. Count slowly.

As you count down...20-19-18-17-16-15...feel your body and mind begin to "awaken." (Your eyes should remain closed).

As you count down...14-13-12-11-10...start to become aware of the sounds and atmosphere around you.

As you count down...9-8-7-6...say to yourself: "When I open my eyes, I will feel simply GREAT! I will feel totally rested and greatly refreshed. When I open my eyes, I will feel terrific. I will be full of energy and will feel greatly refreshed." (All the while you are saying the above, believe it!).

As you count down...5-4-3-2..."feel" yourself starting to feel just great. "Feel" yourself starting to come "alive."

And finally, as you say 1...OPEN YOUR EYES...and immediately GET UP!

How do you feel?

Each S/A Golf Hypnotism session should last about twenty minutes - total. And you should have a session once a day...every day.

Choose a time and place where you would be least likely to be disturbed. It can be before lunch, during your lunch-break, after lunch or sometime during the afternoon or evening. But NOT late at night or after eating a heavy meal (wait a few hours after eating a big meal). You are likely to fall asleep at these times.

Sit in your favorite easy chair, on a bed, couch, in your automobile, or even on the grass. The important thing is that you are comfortable and completely alone.

CHAPTER SIX

How to Use "Booster Sessions"
For Faster Results

In addition to your daily S/A Golf Hypnotism session, you may use two Booster Sessions; once upon arising in the morning, and once just before you retire for the night.

These additional sessions will help you achieve your goal much faster.

Procedure #1

Upon arising in the morning, reach for your list of suggestions.

NOTE: You should write out the suggestions on a separate sheet of paper beforehand...copying them exactly as they appear in this audio book. (This list should also be used for your daily S/A Golf Hypnotism session). This positive action of writing your suggestions out will make your subconscious mind much more receptive to them. After a short time, you will have automatically memorized the suggestions and will no longer need the list.

Continue: Say each suggestion to yourself several times.

This can be done as you prepare for work, as you eat breakfast, or even as you ride to work. The important thing is that you say each suggestion with feeling and belief. See yourself in each situation...reacting just as the suggestion states you will.

Procedure #2

Follow this same procedure just before you go to bed at night.

You may conduct these late night Booster Sessions as you lie in bed...just before you try to fall asleep.

Each Booster Session should last for about ten minutes. Or as long as it takes you to go through your list of suggestions "correctly."

I know the regular sessions and the Booster Sessions may seem like a lot of time-consuming work on your part, but it will pay dividends on the golf course.

Just be patient and do your sessions faithfully and soon your golf buddies will stare in amazement as you make one great shot after another. We guarantee it!

CHAPTER SEVEN

You Are What You "Think" You Are

Why do some men succeed at golf while others fail time and time again? You should know the answer by now. What's the major difference between the man who is at the top of his game and the guy who that's not? What's the difference? The way the man thinks! That's the difference.

Start Thinking Right and You'll Start Playing Right

The man who is on the top of his game thinks in terms of 100% success on the course at all times. While the guy who is not at the top of his game thinks in terms of failure most of the time.

Jim Flick, one of the greatest golf instructors of all time once said, "Golf is 90% mental and the other 10% is mental. In other words, if you learn to control your mind there's no limit to how good of a golfer you can become. And this is exactly what S/A Golf Hypnotism can do for your golf game by controlling your mind.

As a matter of fact, the mental part of golf is so important that all PGA pros have a coach to work with them on their mental game which is the key to playing with confidence, hitting good shots consistently, and shooting lower scores. Also, just about every pro or PGA player agrees that golf is 95-99% mental.

Perhaps, in your case, you've been having a hard time improving your game because you subconsciously EXPECT to have a hard time! When you try to make a good shot, you fail. Why? Because you subconsciously EXPECT to fail. As an example: When you try to avoid a water hazard, you hit the ball in the water a lot of the time. Why? Because you subconsciously EXPECT to hit the ball in the water. And it's the same story when trying to avoid bunkers, trees, hitting the ball out of bounds, etc.

S/A Golf Hypnotism; The Key to Your Success With Golf

Once you begin to change your way of thinking - subconsciously - through S/A Golf Hypnotism - your success on the course will automatically rise...rise...and your handicap will go down...down until you become the golfer you've always wanted to be.

Remember - it isn't really important that you understand WHY these principles work...As long as you know HOW to apply them (as put forth within this audio book).

And remember also - it isn't enough to just think about practicing S/A Golf Hypnotism. You must go ahead and DO IT!

In Conclusion

S/A Golf Hypnotism is working for lots of golfers. Many of who had their doubts when they first heard about these principles. But, they put their doubts aside long enough to give S/A Golf Hypnotism an honest chance.

It didn't take them long to realize how much of a change these principles could make in their golf game.

Maybe you too, don't realize at this time how much of a change S/A Golf Hypnotism can make in your game. If this is the case - let us suggest this: Give it a try. Give it an honest try.

If you will do just that much, we guarantee that your golf game...will take on such a complete change that you will think you were a reborn golfer by some kind of miracle.

But we assure you, it will be no miracle. It will be the mighty force of nature's law working for you. It's all up to you. Good luck. It's been our pleasure talking with you - and remember: "Future success with golf lies within YOUR OWN MIND!"

QUESTIONS AND ANSWERS TIME

The following are some of the questions and answers that seem to always arise whenever the subject of S/A Golf Hypnotism comes up. Look them over. Perhaps we have included questions that you yourself have on your mind.

QUESTION: Why must a person be in a sleep-like condition when applying S/A Golf Hypnotism?

ANSWER: When in this sleep-like condition (altered consciousness), your subconscious mind is much more receptive to ideas or suggestions given to it.

QUESTION: Do I have to practice S/A Golf Hypnotism every single day?

ANSWER: Yes. Missing one day is like missing a month. In order to get full benefit from these principles, they must be practiced every day.

QUESTION: How many minutes to spend on S/A Golf Hypnotism each day?

ANSWER: The more the better. But the average time for a S/A Golf Hypnotism session is about 15 or 20 minutes.

QUESTION: Do I have to practice the booster sessions?

ANSWER: It isn't absolutely necessary...but we do recommend them. The more you give your subconscious mind positive suggestions, the sooner you will reach your goal.

QUESTION: How many weeks, months or years do I have to practice S/A Golf Hypnotism?

ANSWER: Once you begin to use these principles, you won't ever want to stop. It seems to have that effect on most golfers. Besides...remember: "You will never get something for nothing." And you're only kidding yourself if you try. So if you seriously want to become the golfer you've always dreamed about becoming, it's only fair (and required) that you give something in return: your dedication to S/A Golf Hypnotism.

QUESTION: Can I add on suggestions of my own?

ANSWER: Most definitely. At any time, you may add on suggestions of your own or omit some of ours (the ones you feel you do not need) and replace them with yours.

QUESTION: What is the number one cause of failure when practicing S/A Golf Hypnotism?

ANSWER: Disbelief. If you expect S/A Golf Hypnotism to work for you, you MUST have faith in it and believe in what you are doing.

QUESTION: Is it alright to tell others about what I am doing?

ANSWER: No! People enjoy making fun of the other guy. Especially when they do not understand what he's doing. Don't let ignorant, narrow-minded people influence you. Keep your plans to yourself! Don't waste your time, energy and thought on people who have a hard time seeing beyond the tip of their noses.

**Meet, Date, Attract, and Seduce More
Hot & Sexy Women with Our Fantastic Books,
CD's, Pheromone Products, and Cassettes**

Pheromones to Drive Women Wild for Sex:

Liquid Magnet - This powerful pheromone cologne containing a secret rare distilled ancient Hawaiian pheromone formula discovered by scientists, arouses passion in women, drives women wild for sex, and makes them desire you sexually. Order Item #033 - $19.95

CD's to Get You More Love, Romance, Sex:

Mephisto Subliminal Seductions CD's - We call it, "The Lazy Man's Way to Seduce Single Women." All you do is simply insert one of our Subliminal Seduction CD's in your (car-home-portable player) and she thinks she's only hearing music, but she's being secretly and sexually programmed by erotic subliminal messages (concealed under music) to make her uncontrollably want to make mad passionate love to you.

Order Item #075 (Erotic Tropics) - $12.50

Order Item #076 (Lite Rock) - $12.50

Order Item #077 (Country) - $12.50

Order Item #078 (Classical) - $12.50

Order Item #079 (Jazz) - $12.50

Order Item #080 (Early Rock & Roll Oldies) - $12.50

eBooks - (Your eBook will be in the format of a PDF file that will be sent through the U.S. Mail on a CD).

200 Guaranteed Ways to Succeed with Women (eBook) - By learning these proven guaranteed methods, techniques, seduction tips, and specialized knowledge in this "virtual seduction encyclopedia" you can become incredibly successful at meeting, attracting, and seducing single women. Order Item #081 - $4.95

The Easy Way to Get Girls; With S/A Hypnotism (eBook) - Yes, you really can get girls with hypnotism. Order Item #087 - $4.95

1001 Best Pick-Up Lines (eBook) - You will learn 1001 very effective and tested pick-up lines and conversation starters to help you break the ice and have you meeting more women, getting more dates, attracting and seducing more single women, and filling your life with more love, romance, and good times. Order Item #084 - $4.95

The Complete Guide to Meeting Women (eBook) - Meet hot & sexy new women using hundreds of sure-fire techniques for seducing beautiful single women. FREE BONUS included called, "How to Enlarge Your Penis." Order Item #082 - $4.95

How to Pick Up Topless Dancers (eBook) - New amazing eBook reveals how to have your life filled with hot & sexy topless dancers eager to go to bed with you. This is a "must have" book if you go to topless clubs. Order Item #083 - $4.95

A Man's Guide to Women (eBook) - "A Man's Guide to Women" is different than anything you've read before. It's value lies in taking the reader directly to the essentials of being successful with women. It shows you what you have to do to be the type of man that a woman wants to have love her. All the other books tell you what a woman wants from the man she loves. This book tells you how to be the man she loves. This is our best-selling book and highly recommended! Order Item#086 - $4.95

100 Places to Take a Date (eBook) - A lot of men have a hard time thinking of what to do and where to go on a date. If you really want to impress a date and make her fall for you, take her on a unique date she will never forget. Learn about the 100 places to take a date that are guaranteed to win her heart and make her want to become intimate with you. You will learn about romantic date ideas, ideas for a fun date, things to do on a date, date ideas, first date ideas, and much, much more. Order Item#088 - $4.95

How to Talk to Women...A Guide for Tongue-Tied Men (eBook) - Do you get tongue-tied with single women? With the help of this book you won't be anymore - you'll know exactly what to say and how to say it. This ebook provides you with a plan in which the problems have been considered in advance. You will not be trying to figure out what to do (and say) as you go along. It has been thought out for you and laid out clearly for your convenience. It is a packaged plan for the man with romance and sex on his mind. Order Item#089 - $4.95

How to Improve Your Golf with S/A Hypnotism (eBook) - After using this amazing new breakthrough golf improvement system you will know how to drive a golf ball straight, how to swing a golf club, proper way to swing a golf club, how to drive a golf ball further, get rid of your slice, take your game to the next level, putt like a pro, hit your chip, pitch shots dead on the pin from 100 yards in, hit your tee shots long and straight, and lower your handicap 5-10-15 strokes. Order Item#087 - $4.95

Books to Get You Any Woman You Desire:

How to Talk to Women...A Guide for Tongue-Tied Men - Do you get tongue-tied with single women? With the help of this book you won't be any more - you'll know exactly what to say and how to say it. Order Item #031 - $9.95

A Man's Guide to Women – Now any man can meet and date all the single beautiful women he's dreamed of with this amazing best-selling book. * This is our Best-Seller! Please Order Item #034 - $12.95

100 Places to Take a Date – 100 surefire places to take a date that are guaranteed to win a woman's heart and make her want to become intimate with you. Order Item #022 - $6.95

Effective Personal Ads - How to Write Personal Ads or Respond to Personal ads - This tells-all manual will teach you step-by-step everything you need to know on how to score with women using the personals. Order Item #073 - $10.00

Audio Cassettes to Help You Succeed with Women:

The Shy Person's Guide to Successful Dating (cassette) - World-famous author Eric Weber of "How to Pick Up Girls," gives you the secrets of overcoming shyness and finding love, romance with women. The techniques on this audio cassette can literally help any shy man have an active dating life in two short weeks. Order Item #001 - $4.95

How to Find the Love of Your Life in 90 Days or Less (cassettes) - This three hour, double cassette program is the only guide you'll ever need to take control of your love life and find that special someone you've been waiting for. It makes absolutely no difference whether you're young or old, tall or short, heavy or thin, confident or shy...this program will work for you guaranteed! Order Item #055 - $4.95

Please visit our website at: http://www.getgirls.com for more information on these products.

Shipping Charges: United States Orders: 1 item $4.00, each additional item...$1.00

About the Author

Don Diebel (America's #1 Singles Expert) is one of the nation's leading experts on dating and relationships, guest speaker on several TV and radio shows, featured in print interviews, dating consultant, and has helped thousands of men win at the game of love with his phenomenal best-selling books and products.

Also, he is President and owner of Gemini Publishing Company and getgirls.com that specializes in Books, eBooks, Cassettes, CDs, and Pheromone Products to help men successfully, meet, date, and attract women located at: http://www.getgirls.com

Visit his Amazon Store at: https://www.amazon.com/s?me=A38ZQSTGHE2EEQ

Visit his Ebay Store at: http://stores.ebay.com/Dating-Books-CD-DVD-Video-Pheromone

Follow him on Facebook at: https://www.facebook.com/singlesexpert